I0558946

TITLE

10 OBSTACLES TO

YOUR HEALING

ERIC JOSEPH

Book paperback edition: January 2024

Book design, Cover design, and eBook design by mahabulmondol74@gmail.com

Publisher: Amazon KDP TABLE OF CONTENT

Book paperback edition: January 2024

Book design, Cover design, and eBook design by
mahabulmondol74@gmail.com

Publisher: Amazon KDP

PREFACE

Welcome to "10 Obstacles to Your Healing." I wrote this book to illuminate the problems hindering spiritual, mental, emotional, relational, and physical healing. The goal of this book is to give you knowledge and hope, whether you are a Christian looking for advice or someone else looking for ways to deal with problems in your life.

Everyone wants to go on a healing trip. It goes beyond personal, social, and national lines. We all have problems that get in the way of enjoying life to the fullest, being healthy, and being happy. These problems can show up in many ways, such as physical illnesses, mental scars, spiritual unrest, and the issues we face every day.

In these pages, we will talk about ten everyday things that make healing hard. We'll talk about things that can hinder our journey to wholeness, such as sin, a lack of knowledge and understanding, inaction, discipline, faith, and many more. We want to give you helpful information and tools to overcome these problems by using Christian principles, timeless knowledge, and real-life stories as examples.

We plan to bring attention to the issues and suggest answers based on God's Word, faith, love, and resilience. Healing happens in the body, in the spirit, and in the emotions. It's about finding the strength to deal with problems, believing that forgiveness can change things, having strong faith, and living a whole and meaningful life.

Before you start reading "10 Obstacles to Your Healing," we want you to keep an open heart and mind to the ideas of renewal and change. Each part gives you advice and support to find the strength to face your problems head-on and come out on the other side with more clarity, peace, and a renewed sense of purpose. A prayer at each chapter's end can bring miracles in Jesus' name.

May this book be a lighthouse of hope that leads you to heal and encourages you to become the best version of yourself to fully enjoy the whole life God has purposed for you?
With warm regards for your road to recovery,
Eric Joseph

TABLE OF CONTENT

CHAPTER ONE

SIN

Sin can be like a big, heavy wall that keeps us from improving. When we do things against what God wants, that's sin. Like when we lie, hurt others, or choose actions we know are wrong. Sin can wound us physically and mentally, making it hard to be healthy. "The wages of sin are death" (Romans 6:23) in the Bible, which is like a road map for life. In other words, sin can hurt us not only physically but also emotionally and spiritually, making us feel far from God and full of sorrow.

The great news is that even though we sin, there is hope. God cares about us and wants to free us from the weight of our sins by forgiving us. To repent is to turn around and walk away from sin. This means we're sorry for what we did and want God to forgive us. "He is faithful and just, and if we confess our sins, He will forgive us and clean us from all unrighteousness" (1 John 1:9). This promise is vital. It means that God forgives us and cleans us, making us spiritually whole again when we honestly ask for His forgiveness.

Sinning can hurt us in more ways than one. It can hurt our physical health as well. Many health problems can be caused by the stress, guilt, and fear that come from sin. Studies in medicine and psychology have also shown that holding on to bad feelings and guilt can hurt our bodies. Understanding this link between our actions and emotions is very important.

Think of sin as a big bag full of rocks. It gets heavier as we carry it for longer. This is where turning away from sin and asking God to forgive us come in. You can think of it like giving God your big backpack when we tell him about our mistakes and ask for forgiveness. We feel lighter because we don't have to carry around blame and shame. This is a big step toward healing, not just for our mental health. It's also for our physical and emotional health.

Besides that, the Bible tells us how important it is to forgive others. In Matthew 6:14, Jesus said, "For if you forgive others when they sin against you, your heavenly Father will also forgive you." Forgiving other people can also help us get better. Keeping anger and grudges inside can be hard on our hearts and get in the way of our healing. We free ourselves from this load when we forgive, making room for mental and spiritual healing.

To sum up, sin can get in the way of our healing because it affects our minds, hearts, and bodies. But God's love and the gift of healing through turning away from sin are ways to get past this problem. We can go from feeling heavy to feeling light, from guilt to grace, by admitting our sins and asking God to forgive us. We can be mentally, socially, and physically refreshed by taking this vital step toward healing.

- **PRAYER:**Heavenly Father, I understand how much my sins hurt my spiritual and other areas of my life. I come to you in a state of humility.I know that my sin has kept me from being as healed and whole as you want me to be. Lord, give me the courage to face my mistakes, the knowledge to turn away from them, and the humility to ask for your forgiveness. Dear God, please forgive me of all my sins that have been hindering my healing, cleanse me, and make my heart pure. May your grace flow through me, making my spirit whole again, my body renewed, and my path straight. Thank you for freeing me from the bondage of sin in the mighty name of Jesus. Amen.

CHAPTER TWO

LACK OF WISDOM, KNOWLEDGE, AND UNDERSTANDING

Acquiring adequate wisdom, knowledge, andunderstanding can be like having a plan or a flashlight to help you find your way through a dark forest. It makes it harder for us to get better. Don't worry, though; there is hope! Let's look at how getting wisdom, knowledge, and understanding can help us get healthier and happier.

Being wise is like having a golden chest full of information. It helps us pick healthy things to do. "The beginning of wisdom is this: get wisdom. Even if it costs all you have, get understanding" (Proverbs 4:7). Knowledge is so essential that it's worth working to find it.

Where do we get this knowledge, then? One way is to pray. Prayer is like conversing with the most intelligent person in the world. We can ask Him to help us understand and make sense of our health. It says in the Bible book of James, "If any of you lacks wisdom, you should ask God, who gives freely to all without finding fault, and it will be given to you" (16:5). This shows that God is ready to help us become wise if we ask.

Scripture is another excellent source of knowledge, just like God's book of life rules. There are stories, tips, and lessons in it that can help us make intelligent choices about our health. 1 Corinthians 6:19–20 says, "Do you not know that your bodies are temples of the Holy Spirit, who is in you and whom you received from God? You are not your own;

you were bought at a price. So, honor God with your bodies." This reminds us that our bodies are gifts from God and should be taken care of.

Making smart choices is also very important. It's like following a map to get somewhere. We can talk to doctors and other health workers for advice and gather information to help us make good decisions for our health. Proverbs 15:22 says, "Plans fail for lack of counsel, but with many advisers, they succeed." This verse tells us to get help and information before making significant choices, especially those affecting our health.

Having enough wisdom, information, and understanding can help our healing. But we can overcome this problem by praying for knowledge, reading the Bible, and making choices based on our experience. Remember that you're not going through this trip by yourself. God is always ready to help you get better health and a better future. Let's take those steps together to become wise and heal!

- **PRAYER:** Heavenly Father, I come to you knowing that I need your wisdom, knowledge, and understanding, especially regarding my health and healing. I'll admit that sometimes, my ignorance has caused me to make bad decisions for my health. Lord, I humbly ask for your help and insight. Please give me the insight to make intelligent choices, the ability to put my health first, and the knowledge to get through life's challenges. Please give me your spiritual wisdom and show me the way to health.

Communing with you and your word will teach me how to care for my body, mind, and spirit in a way that honors you. May your knowledge help me find my way to total health. I pray in the name of Jesus. Amen.

CHAPTER THREE

LACK OF ACTION

Not doing anything is like having a cake recipe but never making the cake. You already have everything you need to make the cake, but you need to mix it. We need to do more than know what to do to heal; we need to take the steps to make it happen.

The Bible talks a lot about how important it is to do things. James 2:17 says, "Faith by itself if it is not accompanied by action, is dead." This means having faith is great, but you have to implement it. It would help if you did things to keep the healing process going. Faith is like the spark that starts it.

To better understand this, let's look at a real-life case. Let's say someone is struggling with their health and weight. They may know that to be healthier, they need to eat better and work out more often. But their health will only get better if they do something about it. They need to eat healthy foods and work out regularly. The act of doing something is what starts the healing process.

Here's one more example. Think about someone hurting emotionally because of something that happened in the past. They may believe that they can get better, but the pain may keep getting worse if they don't do something to get help or therapy. They can find peace and healing when actively seeking help and taking steps to improve.

You don't have to make massive changes immediately because you're taking action. There are easy things you can do to start, like choosing veggies over a candy bar or calling a friend to talk about how you feel. These small things can make a big difference in your health and well-being.

Look at a solid biblical example of how to help someone get better. In the New Testament, there is a story about a woman who had a problem with bleeding for twelve years. She had heard about Jesus and thought that she could be healed if she could touch the bottom of His robe. Because of her faith, she did what she did. She reached out into the crowd and brushed the coat of arms of Jesus. She was healed right away. Jesus knew she had faith in him and told her, "Daughter, your faith has healed you. Go in peace and be free from your pain" (Mark 5:34). This story tells us that when we act out of faith, fantastic healing can happen.

Getting over an addiction is another real-life example of taking action. Someone who is having trouble with addiction might want to get away from it. Though they may believe they can get through it, they will only truly be healed when they decide to get help, join a support group, or start a rehab program. The choice to face their problem and make changes is what can help them recover and heal for good.

Faith and deed go together in both of these cases. They work together to make it possible for people to heal. As we begin our paths to healing, let's remember how important it is to be vigilant. Let's put our faith into action, like the woman who touched Jesus' clothing, and trust that we can be healed if we are determined to change.

To sum up, healing takes more than just praying or waiting for it to happen. It would help if you took action, were ready to make changes, and promised to stick to your word. Remember, even small steps can add up to significant growth. Let's do more than talk about healing. Let's make it happen in our own lives. That very first step is the start of your healing journey!

- **Prayer:** Lord, I come to you with a spirit ready to act and a heart that wants to be healed. I'll be honest: I've let laziness and fear stop me from taking the steps I needed to get better at times. I give up my fears and worries to you today. Please give me the courage to step out in faith, make the changes I need to make, and take an active role in my healing journey. May your strength help me take those crucial steps toward health and happiness, knowing that with your help, each move brings me closer to the life you promised me would be complete. I pray in the name of Jesus. Amen.

CHAPTER FOUR

LACK OF DISCIPLINE

Being disciplined can be like trying to steer a boat without an oar if we don't follow through with our plans. We may know where we want to go, but if we don't, we'll float along. Discipline is essential to healing because it helps us maintain physical and mental health. Let's talk about why discipline is necessary and how to improve it.

In the Bible, discipline is often tied to being wise and having self-control. "Like a city whose walls are broken through is a person who lacks self-control," says Proverbs 25:28. This tells us that discipline keeps us safe from things that could hurt our health and well-being.

When it comes to our food, we need to be very disciplined. Our foodsignificantly affects our health, like putting suitable gas in your car to make it run smoothly. Being strict about what we eat can help us stay at a healthy weight, avoid getting sick, and feel more energized. It means making wise choices, like eating lots of fruits and veggies and not too many sugary or sour foods.

Discipline is also essential when it comes to exercise. The Bible says that the Holy Spirit lives in our bodies (1 Corinthians 6:19). A way to honor God is to care for our bodies by working out regularly. Regarding exercise, discipline means setting aside time to do something, even if we don't like it. The point is to make an action you enjoy a regular part of your life.

Health in the mind is just as important as health in the body. Discipline means dealing with worry, being thankful, and keeping a good attitude. "Finally, brothers and sisters, whatever is true, whatever is noble, whatever is right, whatever is pure, whatever is lovely, whatever is admirable—if anything is excellent or praiseworthy, think about such things." (Philippians 4:8). This verse reminds us that our thoughts have power and that keeping a positive, disciplined mind is essential.

How, then, can we get more control in these areas? First, make your goals clear. We need to know where we're going like a ship's captain calculating a route. Setting clear goals helps us stay on track when trying to eat better, work out daily, or manage our mental health.

Next, it's essential to make a plan. Like a builder following a plan, we need a road map to help us get where we want to go. This could mean planning meals, working out, or setting aside time to be aware and rest.

Another effective way to plan is to ask others to hold you accountable. You can stay on track if you tell a friend or family member about your goals and ask them to support you and check your progress. Having a co-pilot to ensure you stay on course is like having one.

Finally, remember that discipline isn't about perfection but getting better. Things could go wrong along the way, but that's okay. It's essential to get back on track and keep going. Discipline becomes a habit over time, and taking care of your health and recovery becomes second nature.

It is important to remember that discipline will help us get and stay healthy in our lives. We can respect our bodies as temples of the Holy Spirit and live healthier, more meaningful lives by being strict about what we eat, how much we exercise, and how we feel mentally. It takes work, but the benefits of better health and well-being are well worth it. To get better, let's make plans, set goals, hold each other accountable, and remember that progress, not perfection, is the key to success on this path.

- **PRAYER:** Heavenly Father, I humbly admit that I need to be more disciplined in all parts of my life, especially regarding my health and healing. I'm sorry to say that my lack of control has slowed me down and stopped me from living the entire life you want for me. Dear Lord, I give you my flaws and struggles. Please give me the willpower and self-control to form good habits, treat my body as your home, and work on my mental and spiritual discipline. Please help me keep going even when things get complicated because discipline is the way to freedom and health. In the name of Jesus, I pray that you will give me the strength to live an orderly life that brings you glory. Amen.

CHAPTER FIVE

LACK OF FAITH

When we don't have faith, it can be like trying to sail a boat without wind. Faith is what moves us forward on our path to health. Doubt can get in the way of bringing God's healing kindness. Faith is a strong force that can cause it. Let's talk about how to improve our faith and how important it is in the healing process.

Jesus often talked about how important faith is for healing in the Bible. In Matthew 9:22, He told a woman who had been sick for a long time, "Do not be afraid, daughter; your faith has healed you." This shows that faith is more than just an opinion; it is a living thing that can bring healing.
Think about someone who is dealing with a problematic sickness. They may feel scared and stressed. But faith is like a light in the dark; it gives us hope and peace of mind. It means trusting God's healing power is more vital than any illness or problem we face.

The book of Mark has a strong story about hope. A father took his sick child to Jesus and said, "I believe; help me get over my doubt!" (Mark 9:24). The Father's honest statement helps us remember that we can ask God for help even when our faith is weak. God knows we have questions and is ready to help us have more faith if we ask.

We can also read Mark 5:25–34, which tells the story of the woman who touched the bottom of Jesus' robe. She had been hurting for twelve years, but her faith kept her going, and she thought that feeling Jesus' clothes would heal her. He told her, "Your faith has healed you. Go in peace." So, how can we keep our faith in the healing process alive and robust? To begin, one must pray and seek a closer connection with God. It's like talking to a friend you trust when you pray. God can work in our minds when we tell Him our worries, fears, and dreams.

Another way to improve your faith is to read and think about the Word of God. Romans 10:17 says, "Faith comes from hearing the message, and the message is heard through the word about Christ." The Bible contains stories about faith, miracles, and God's promises that can help us heal.

Being in a group of believers who help each other can also boost our faith. Being a part of a faith group can give us the support and motivation to keep our faith strong, just like a warm breeze can lift a kite into the air.

Finally, it's essential to be patient. It may take time to heal, and our trust may be tested. Remember, though, that. God's timing is always right, and He works for our good.

Finally, faith is an integral part of the healing process. It's about having faith in God's healing power, even when things look bad. Reading about people's faith in the Bible and trying to get closer to God through praying, reading the Bible, and being in a faith-based group can help increase our faith. Trusting that God's healing grace will work even in the most challenging circumstances lets us believe His light can bring repair and health.

- **PRAYER:** "Dear Lord, I come to you with a heavy heart and doubts about my faith." I'll be honest: There have been times when I didn't believe in your healing power. I put my worries at your feet today and ask for unwavering trust. Lord, strengthen my faith and help me eliminate any doubts that have taken root in my mind. Teach me to believe what you say, not what I think I know, and rest knowing that your healing is always available. I pray this in the name of Jesus: Give me the firm faith to move mountains and the patience to wait for your suitable time. Amen.

CHAPTER SIX

SPIRITUAL WARFARE

A real fight is happening in the spiritual world, even though it sounds like something from a fairy tale. Soldiers need armor to keep them safe, and we need spiritual armor to protect ourselves from evil spiritual forces that get in the way of our health. Discuss spiritual warfare, its importance, and how we can deal with these problems.

In the book of Ephesians, the Bible talks about spiritual war. The Bible says in Ephesians 6:12, "For our struggle is not against flesh and blood, but against the rulers, against the authorities, against the powers of this dark world and the spiritual forces of evil in the heavenly realms." This verse tells us that forces outside of ourselves can try to bring us down.

Negative feelings and thoughts are one way that spiritual conflict can change us. It's like a storm cloud that keeps us from seeing the happiness and peace in our lives. These evil thoughts can make us question God's love, ourselves, and our worth.

Temptation is another way that spiritual war takes place. It's hard to say no to a sweet treat, and the same is true for spiritual pressures. They can keep us from making good choices for our minds and bodies. One example is that it might make us want to pick up bad habits or do bad things.

How, then, can we find and get rid of mental problems that are stopping us from healing? Awareness of these negative impacts is the first thing that needs to be done. Like a good detective, we must think about our thoughts, feelings, and behaviors. When we feel bad or are tempted, we can stop and ask ourselves if it's coming from an unhealthy spiritual source.

In spiritual warfare, prayer is a handy tool. Like texting a friend, you trust to ask for help, people who pray are talking to God, and He can give us the power and protection we need. Paul tells us in Ephesians 6:18 to "pray in the Spirit at all times with all kinds of prayers and requests."

The Bible also talks about protection for the heart. Our spiritual armor keeps us safe in spiritual fights, just like a knight's armor does in battle. These defense pieces are talked about in Ephesians 6:13–17. Some of them are the helmet of salvation, the righteousness breastplate, and the faith shield. These pieces help us stand firm when evil spirits try to hurt us.

Last, we must remember that we are not fighting this battle alone. Being in a group of believers who support and encourage us can give us strength and comfort. We can discuss our problems, pray for each other, and stand against evil spiritual forces.

To sum up, a spiritual battle is a real problem that can affect our health. These problems can be solved by realizing negative spiritual influences, praying, putting on our spiritual armor, and asking for help from our faith group. We can win the spiritual war and move forward on our path to healing, just like troops win fights by planning and being strong.

- **PRAYER:** Heavenly Father, I stand in your presence, knowing I am in a spiritual battle. I'll be honest: There have been times when I felt like destructive spiritual forces were taking over my life. Today, I give up my power and safety to your holy authority. I put on my spiritual gear to stand firm against the enemy's plans. Please give me the wisdom to see the dark forces trying to stop my healing journey and fight them. Please empower me with your spirit. Your word declaresthat he who is in me is more powerful than the forces of darkness and evil in this world. I pray that I will win the spiritual fight in the mighty name of Jesus. With you by my side, I claim victory today. Amen.

CHAPTER SEVEN

UNRESOLVED TRAUMA

Trauma that hasn't been dealt with can be like having a big backpack full of rocks. We take hurt and painful memories from the past with us, which can make it hard for us to heal. Let's discuss how trauma that hasn't been dealt with can affect our health and how faith and forgiveness can help.

In the Bible, there's a story about Joseph, whose brothers sold him into slavery, which caused him a lot of pain. But in Genesis 50:20, Joseph said, "You meant to hurt me, but God meant it for good to save many lives." This story shows us that even in the worst times, God can heal and change situations in our lives.

Trauma that hasn't been dealt with can keep us stuck in the past. It's like a chain that stops us from going forward. These wounds can appear as anger, fear, or even health problems. On the other hand, mercy is the key that lets us go free. Jesus said in Matthew 6:14–15, "For if you forgive others when they sin against you, your heavenly Father will also forgive you. But your Father will not forgive your sins if you do not forgive others." This shows that to forgive means to let go of the past and receive God's forgiveness in return.

Forgiving someone doesn't mean we agree or forget about what they did. It has to do with letting go of hurts from the past and the anger and sadness they cause. It's not always easy to do this, but it's crucial for our healing.

Being a Christian is a big part of getting over past hurts. It helps us find our way out of the darkness of pain like a light. And when we believe that God loves us and can fix us, we can face our past and look forward to a better future.

Remember that getting better after a traumatic event takes time. It takes time and often means getting professional help or support from caring people. It takes time for a broken bone to heal; the same is true for our mental and spiritual wounds.

Self-compassion is just as crucial for healing from pain as faith and forgiveness. We must be kind to ourselves and know that feeling hurt and sad is okay. Just like a hurt animal needs care, we must give ourselves time and support to heal.

In conclusion, pain that isn't dealt with can make healing much harder. But we can get over the effects of past hurts by forgiving others, believing in God's power to heal, getting help, and being kind to ourselves. Like Joseph, we can find meaning and healing in our pain and suffering. This will help us move toward a better and more hopeful future.

- **PRAYER**: Dear Lord, I come to you with a heavy heart from trauma that I haven't dealt with. I'm sorry, but both seen and hidden hurts inside me have kept me captive for far too long. I bring these problems to your throne today and ask for the healing touch only you can give. I have the faith to believe that your love can change things, the courage to face my past, and the strength to forgive. Lord, heal my scars and set me free from the chains of suffering. I know that your love and power are more than enough to heal the wounds in my body, soul, and, spirit today in the mighty name of JesusI pray, Amen.

CHAPTER EIGHT

UNHEALTHY RELATIONSHIPS

Relationships that are unhealthy, controlling, or emotionally harmful can get in the way of our healing. It is like big rocks blocking a clear, smooth road. First, let's talk about why these relationships can be troublesome and how we can deal with them by following Christian values of love and freedom.

In the Bible, God talks about love and how important it is to keep relationships healthy. These verses from 1 Corinthians 13:4–7 say thatlove is patient and kind. It doesn't envy, it doesn't boast, and it isn't proud. It doesn't dishonor others, isn't self-seeking, doesn't get angry quickly, and doesn't keep track of wrongs. Love doesn't delight in evil but rejoices with the truth. It always protects, trusts, hopes, and perseveres." They stress that love should be a strength and not a source of pain.

There are often poisonous signs in relationships that aren't good, which can significantly affect our health. These signs include constant criticism, control, manipulation, or abuse of emotions. Something is missing if a relationship always makes us sad, nervous, or tired.

Setting and sticking to healthy limits when dealing with unhealthy relationships is essential. Proverbs 4:23 says, "Above all else, guard your heart, for everything you do flows from it." This verse shows how important it is to protect our emotional and mental health by setting limits that keep us safe.

Jesus said in Matthew 18:15, "If your brother or sister sins, go and point out their fault, just between the two of you. If they listen to you, you have won them over." Being open and honest with each other is vital to fixing unhealthy relationships.

If, however, the destructive patterns don't change despite your efforts, you may need to break away from the toxic relationship. It's important to know that stepping away from a relationship that's hurting you is not an act of not liking them; it's a way to protect yourself.

Also, surrounding yourself with a Christian group that supports you can be accommodating when dealing with bad situations. Other Christians can help you through these challenging situations by giving you advice, support, and prayers. Ecclesiastes 4:9–10 says, "Two are better than one because they have a good return for their labor. If either of them falls, one can help the other up." This verse shows how important it is to have friends and help each other.

Finally, it's essential to understand that bad relationships can get in the way of our healing. By knowing the signs of toxic relationships, setting and talking about healthy limits, and getting help from a loving Christian community, we can deal with these problems while following the Bible's teachings on love and care. Do not forget that God wants us to have healthy, caring relationships, and it is okay to protect yourself when you are in a bad relationship.

Prayer: Heavenly Father, I come to you knowing that bad relationships have hurt my life and my path to healing. I'm sorry to say that for too long I've let unhealthy relationships harm my health. Today, I give these situations over to you. Please grant me the discernment to identify unhealthy bonds, the courage to set boundaries, and the strength to seek healing for myself and those who have caused harm. Lead me toward healthy, nurturing connections that reflect your love and grace. I pray that you will restore my relationships and heal my heart, trusting that your guidance will lead me to the freedom and wholeness I seek today in Jesus' name. Amen.

CHAPTER NINE

UNCONFESSED SINS

The sin we don't admit can hold us back like a heavy anchor, stopping us from going forward on our path to healing. Let's examine the idea of unconfessed sin and see why getting better can be challenging. We can be accessible by confessing our sins, repenting, and asking God to forgive us.

It is clear from the Bible how important it is to admit faults and turn away from them. If we confess our sins, 1 John 1:9 says, "He is faithful and just and will forgive our sins and clean us from all unrighteousness." This verse tells us that God is ready and willing to forgive and clean us from all unrighteousness when we ask him to.

The sins we don't admit can make us feel guilty and ashamed. It's like having a big load on our shoulders, which makes it hard to stand tall and move around quickly. The weight of guilt can hurt our mental and spiritual health and make it harder to heal.

Admitting your sins is a vital part of getting better. In other words, it's like saying we went off track and asking for help to get back on track. When we admit our sins, we let go of our guilt and let God's forgiveness and healing kindness come in.

Another essential part of dealing with unconfessed sin is repentance. Not just saying "I'm sorry," but making a sincere promise to stop doing bad things and try to live a life that follows God's rules. Acts 3:19 tells us to "repent and turn to God so that your sins may be forgiven and times of refreshing may come from the Lord." When we repent, our lives are renewed in a refreshing and new way.

It takes faith and humility to ask God to forgive you. It's like knowing that if we tell a loved one we're sorry, they will welcome us back with open arms. God can forgive us without any conditions, but we must ask for it.

The sin we don't admit can also hurt our relationship with God. Like a wall, it keeps us from getting to Him. Isaiah 59:2 says, "But your sins have separated you from your God; they have hidden his face from you so that he will not hear." When we admit our transgressions and ask for forgiveness, we remove that block and reconnect with God. This lets His healing presence flow into our lives.

Unconfessed sin can make it much harder to get better. We can eliminate our guilt and shame, fix our relationship with God, and let His healing and grace come to us if we admit our sins, say sorry, and ask for His forgiveness. Remember that God will always forgive you, and it's never too late to return to Him and get the peace and healing He gives.

- **PRAYER:**Dear Lord, I humbly come to you, knowing that my unconfessed sins have interrupted my healing journey. I'm sorry that I have sometimes hidden my sins and let guilt and shame hold me back. Today, I put these transgressions at the feet of Jesus and believe that you will forgive me. Please give me the courage and humility to say I'm sorry and the faith to accept your forgiveness. Dear God, please wash me clean and make my heart pure. Let your loving care heal me, make me feel better, and give me new hope. May the freedom come from knowing you forgive me and that your love covers all my sins in the name of Jesus. Amen.

CHAPTER TEN

NEGATIVE THOUGHT PATTERNS

Negative thoughts and doubts about ourselves or the Word of God can be like dark clouds that keep the healing light from reaching us. Let's address how these mental blocks can get in our way of healing and look at some powerful and productive ways to eliminate them, such as Bible affirmations and mind-renewal practices.

The Bible tells us that our thoughts have power. Proverbs 23:7 says, "As a man thinks in his heart, so is he." This reminds us that our thoughts make us who we are and determine what we do. We can question ourselves, our worth, and God's love for us when we think negatively.

Negative thoughts, like self-doubt, happen a lot. We hear a whisper that tells us we're not good enough, not worthy of healing, or unable to change all the time. Sometimes, these thoughts are so strong that they stop us from doing what we need to do to get better.

Awareness is the first step in changing negative thought habits into more positive ones. Awareness of these thoughts gives us the power to question and change them, like turning on a light in a dark room.

Affirmations from the Bible are constructive. We can change our evil thoughts with good Bible verses. When we feel uncertainty about ourselves, we can say things like "I am fearfully and wonderfully made" (Psalm 139:14) or "I can do all things through Christ who strengthens me" (Philippians 4:13). These statements help us remember how valuable and vital we are in God.

The Bible talks about renewing the mind, which means changing our thoughts. The Bible tells us in Romans 12:2, "Do not conform to the pattern of this world, but be transformed by the renewing of your mind." We can be transformed by letting God's Word shape our thoughts and views.

Another critical approach is prayer. Giving our evil thoughts to God in prayer is like giving our worries to a caring friend. Philippians 4:6-7 says, "Do not be anxious about anything, but in every situation, by prayer and petition, with thanksgiving, present your requests to God. And the peace of God, which transcends all understanding, will guard your hearts and minds in Christ Jesus."

It's also helpful to get help from a Christian group. A ladder can help us get up a steep hill, and a group of Christians can do the same for us by giving us support, holding us accountable, and praying as we fight negative thought patterns.

Finally, negative thought patterns and self-doubt can get in the way of our health. These thoughts can't hold us back if we are aware of them. We should use biblical promises, renew our minds through God's Word, pray, and ask for help from our faith community. Don't forget that God gave you worth and a reason when He made you. You can get through these problems through Him and experience His healing and change.

- **PRAYER:** Dear Heavenly Father, I come to you because I know these negative thought patterns have held me back for too long. I'm sorry to say that these thoughts have slowed my recovery and limited what I can do. Today, I give these harmful patterns to your power to change my thoughts. Please give me the strength to fight these evil thoughts and replace them with your word. Fill my mind with the truths in your word, and help me think again in line with your perfect plan. I pray that you will refresh my mind, heal my spirit, and give me the freedom to live a life full of good thoughts and unshakable faith in your promises in Jesus' name. Amen

CONCLUSION

As we end "10 Obstacles to Your Healing," I want to leave you with a strong word that will make you want to do something even more. We've discussed the spiritual, mental, emotional, relational, and spiritual problems that might stop you from healing. You now know how sin, not having enough knowledge, wisdom, or understanding, not taking action, not being disciplined, not having faith, spiritual warfare, unresolved trauma, and unhealthy relationships can get in the way of your growth. But now it's time to do something.

It's no longer okay to just put up with these problems. Now is the time to get above them, beat them, and get away from their chains. You should not be a victim of your situation; instead, you should be a winner through Christ.
I want you to pray to God first, ask Him to help, and give you strength. He is your rock, your source of knowledge, and your hope. You will find the strength to face these problems head-on in His presence.

First, write down the exact problems that have been stopping you. Think about the times in your life when you've felt stuck or hurt. Figure out the bad habits and trends that have prevented you from improving.

Next, promise to deal with these problems one at a time. Just keep taking those little steps. Remember that the goal is not perfection but growth. Get help from a professional, like a therapist, for ongoing stress or a doctor for physical healing.

Read God's Word and make faith statements to yourself. Instead of evil thoughts, think about the promises in the Bible. Let God's truth shine brightly on you, driving out the darkness of doubt and hopelessness.

Get involved with a Christian group that loves and supports you. Find Christians who can hold you accountable and give you support. They can walk this journey with you. Remember that you're not fighting this battle by yourself. Lastly, always keep sight of the picture of yourself getting healed. Keep your eyes on what God has to offer: hope and healing. Use the possibility of a better, more robust, and more complete life to propel you.

Finally, I want you to know that your health is a dream and a reality you can achieve. Even though the problems felt big, your faith and drive are stronger. You have all the power of God inside you. So, leave these pages with a firm resolve, ready to face and overcome these problems, and accept the healing and completeness God has planned for you. Your trip begins now. Do not wait any longer; act now and enter the rich life waiting for you.

- **PRAYER:** Heavenly Father, as I finish reading "10 Obstacles to Your Healing," I am amazed by your unending love and healing power. Thank you for giving me the knowledge and strength to get past these problems and start a path to healing and wholeness. With a grateful heart, I offer a prayer today, giving you control of my past, present, and future. May your healing hands continue to rest upon my life, show me the way, make me feel better, and lead me to a life filled with your love and purpose. I receive strength to keep walking to the path of healing in the name of Jesus, Amen.

If this book has helped you, please write a review on Amazon.com so others can experience the same. Many thanks!

Thank you for taking this journey with me through "10 Obstacles to Your Healing." If these words have resonated with you, I invite you to explore more of my writings of inspiring books on Amazon that delve into spirituality, counseling, personal growth, and the human experience. Books include Saved but Struggling, Well but Wounded: The Benefits of Professional Christian Counseling, Be Made Whole: The 5 Dimensions of Healing, and What Do You Do After You Have Prayed? Your ongoing support means the world to me.